**Welcome to Study and Color
This book focuses on the Korean alphabet.**

Hangul is the native alphabet of the Korean language. There are 14 Consonants and 10 vowels.

When writing in Korean you must remember the current **stroke order**.

When writing Hangul, start in the upper left of the letter and move left to right, top to bottom

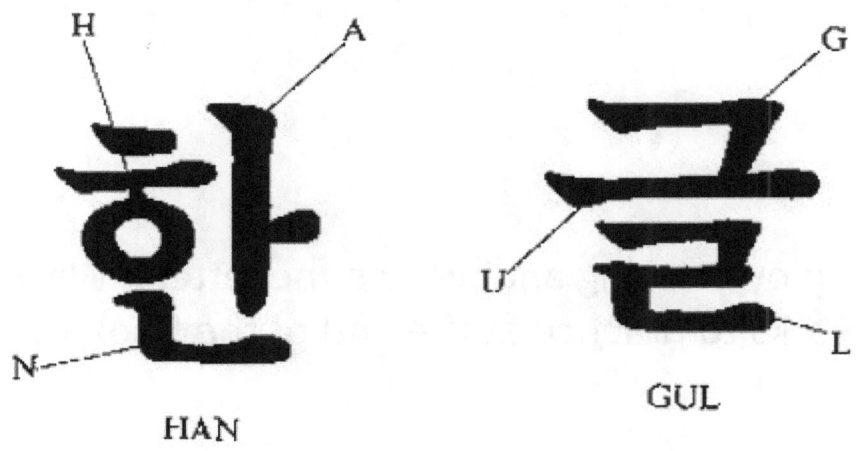

HAN

GUL

●Consonants:

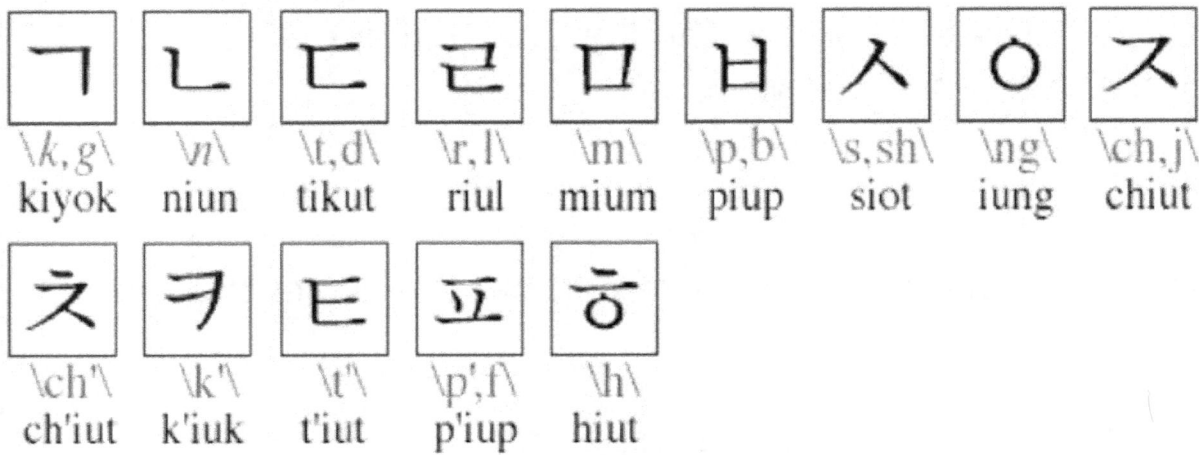

●Vowels:

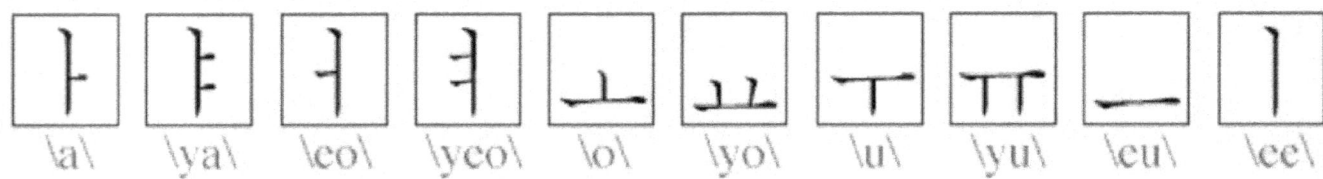

Now it is your turn ! Enjoy coloring and writing the letters. We will provide a couple of works to practice at the end of the book !

Pronounced kiyok
Written in English as k or g

Practice writing the letter 10 times

Pronounced niun
Written in English as n

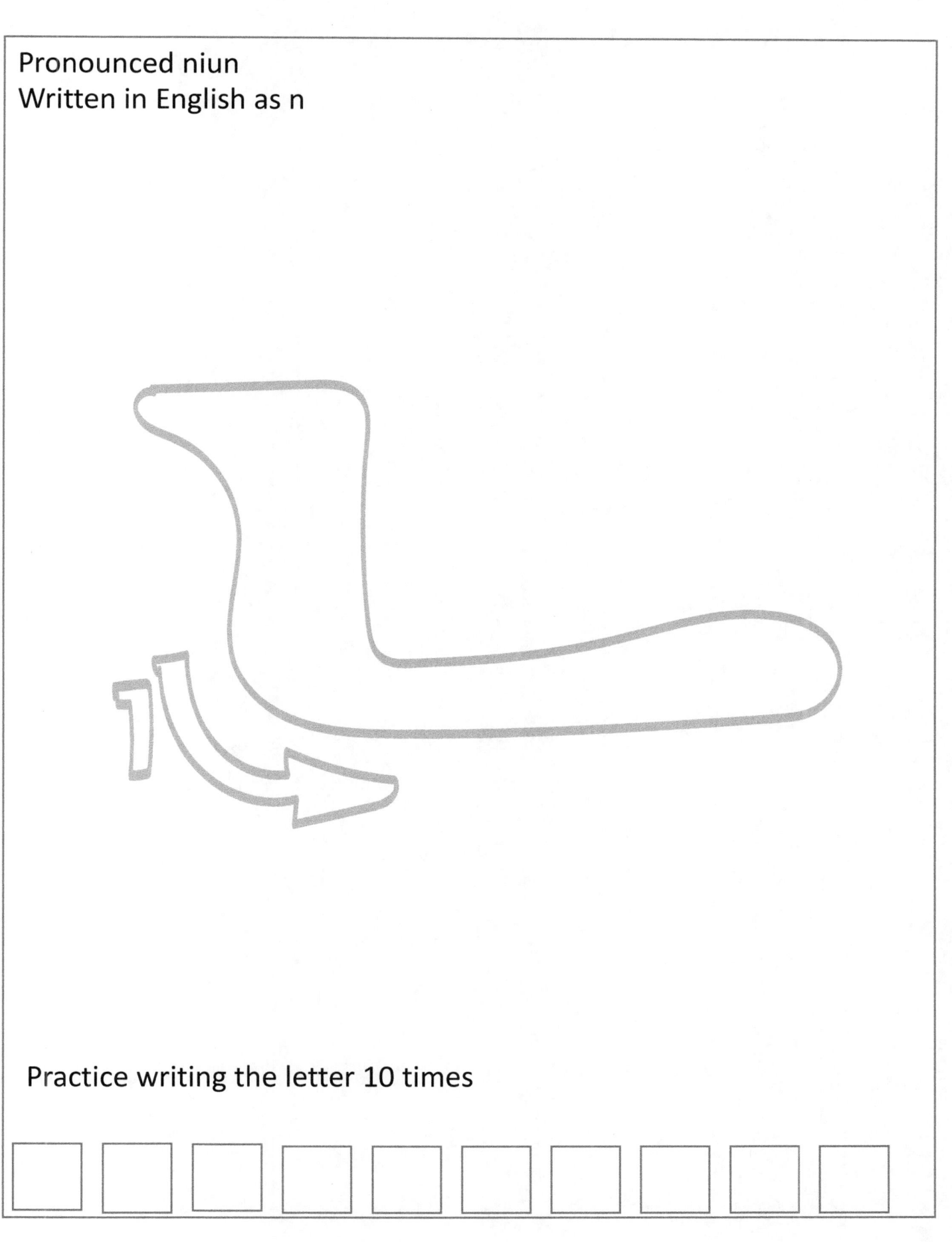

Practice writing the letter 10 times

Pronounced tikut
Written in English as t or d

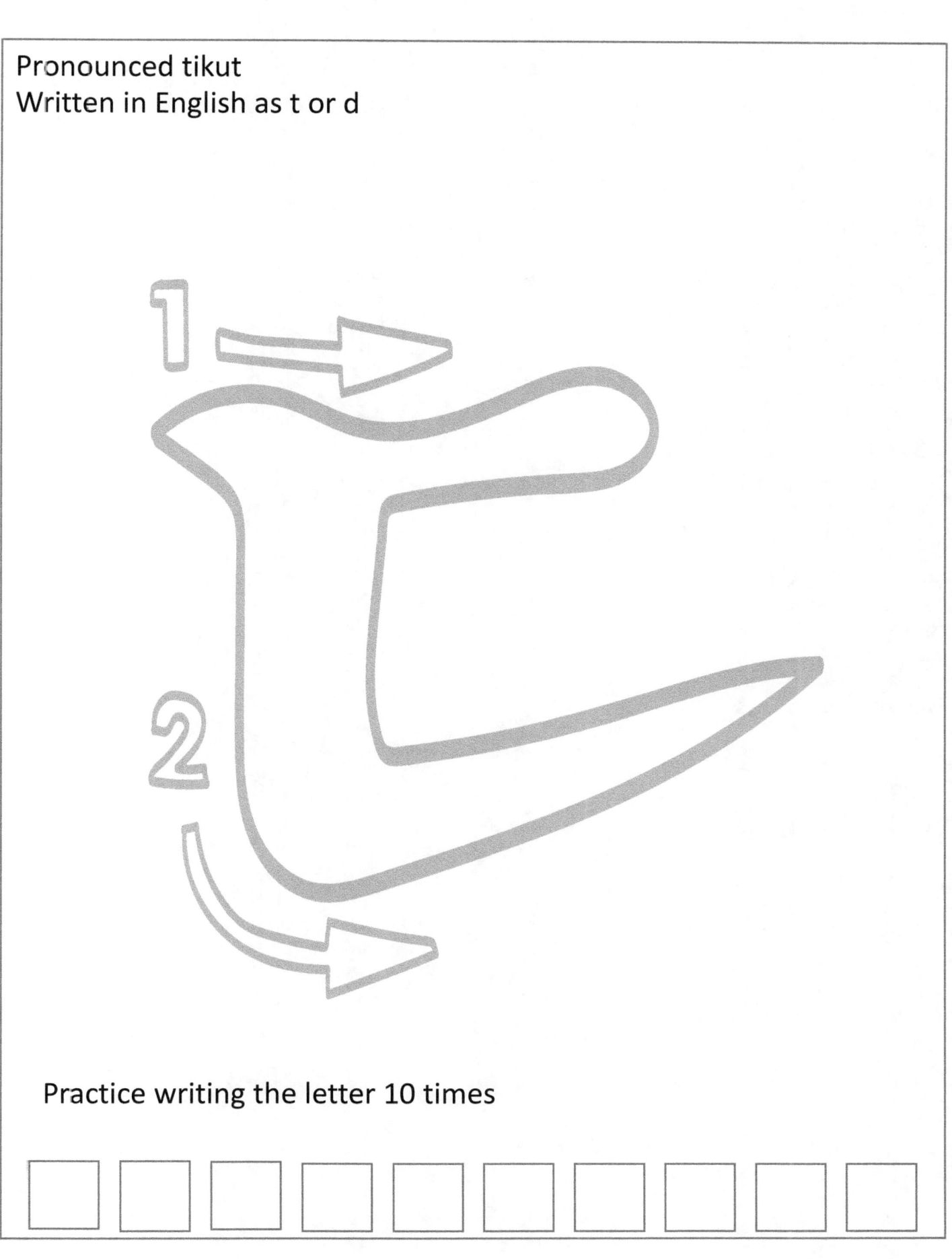

Practice writing the letter 10 times

Pronounced riul
Written in English as r or l

Practice writing the letter 10 times

Pronounced mium
Written in English as m

Practice writing the letter 10 times

Pronounced piup
Written in English as p or b

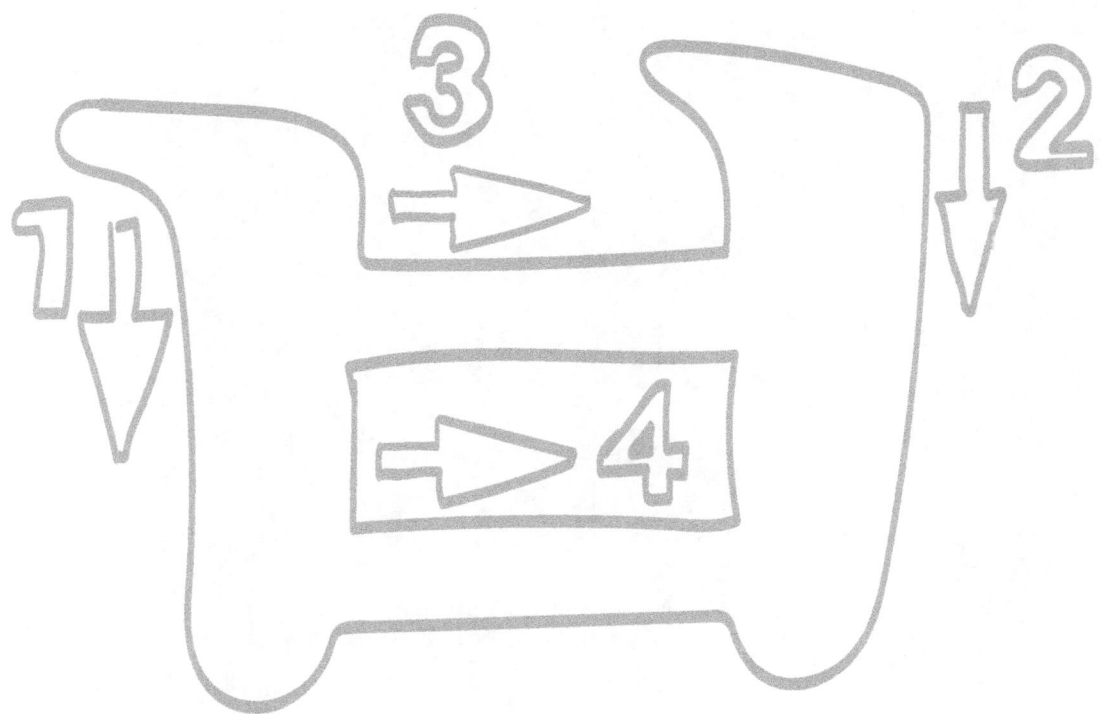

Practice writing the letter 10 times

Pronounced siot
Written in English as s or sh

Practice writing the letter 10 times

Pronounced iung
Written in English as ng

Practice writing the letter 10 times

Pronounced chiut
Written in English as ch or j

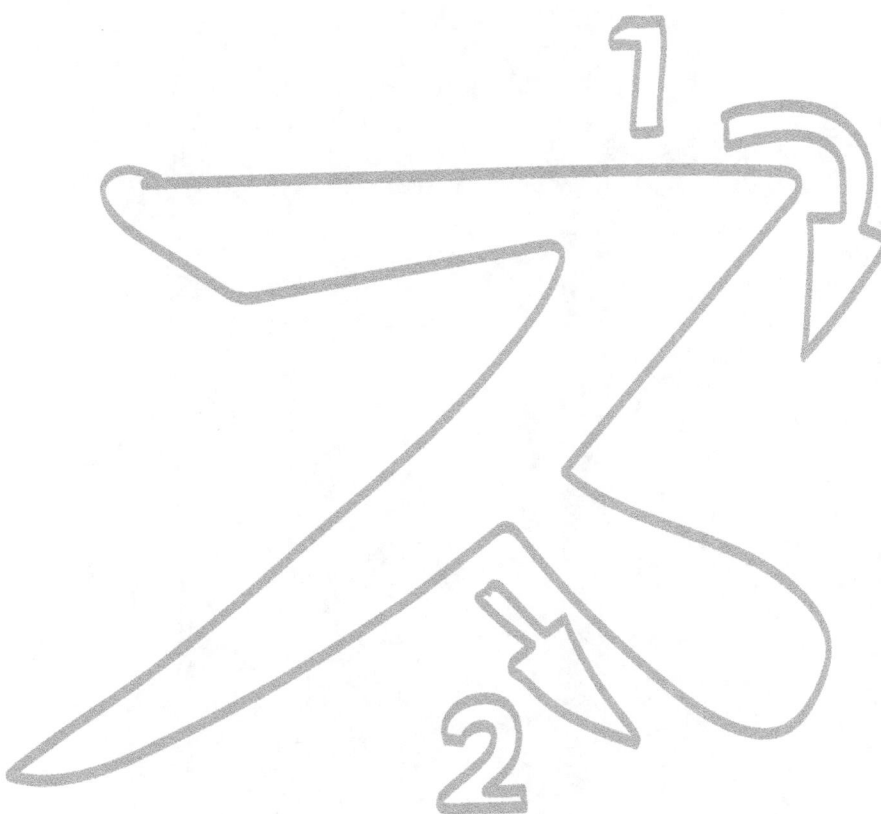

Practice writing the letter 10 times

Pronounced ch'iut
Written in English as ch'

Practice writing the letter 10 times

Pronounced k'iuk
Written in English as k'

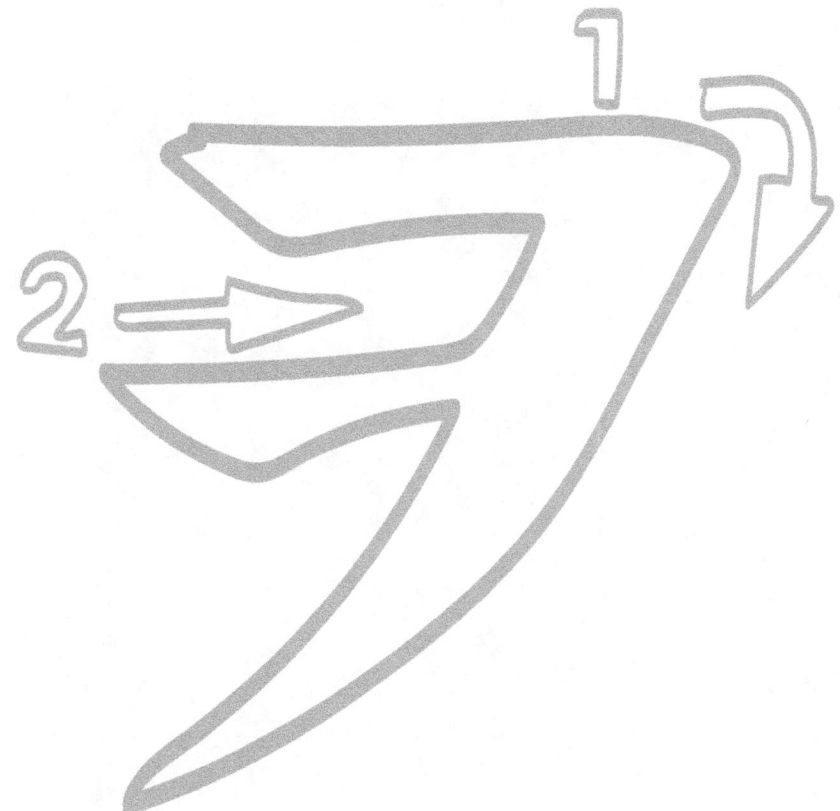

Practice writing the letter 10 times

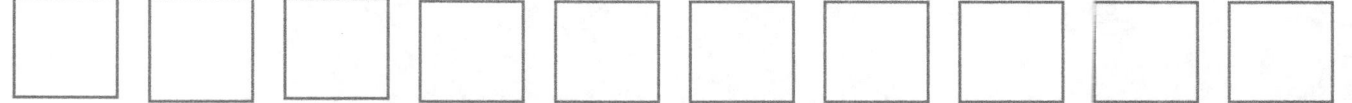

Pronounced t'uit
Written in English as t'

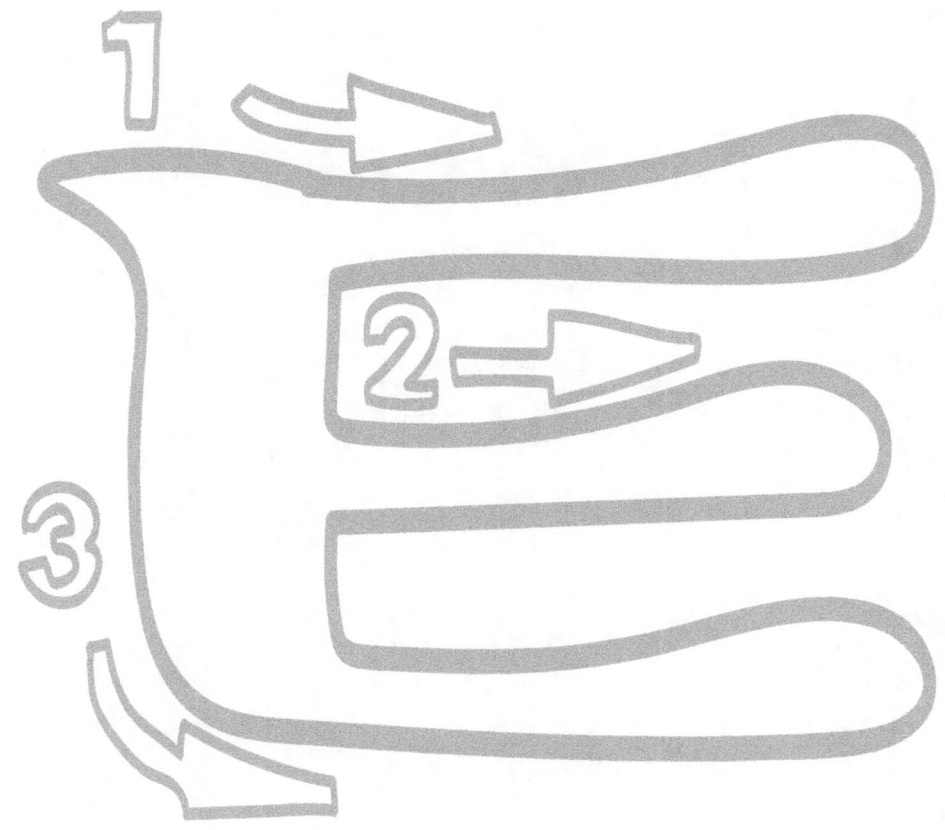

Practice writing the letter 10 times

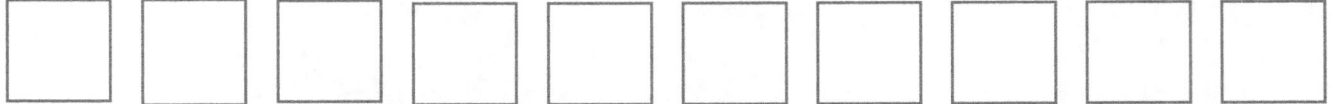

Pronounced p'iup
Written in English as p' or f

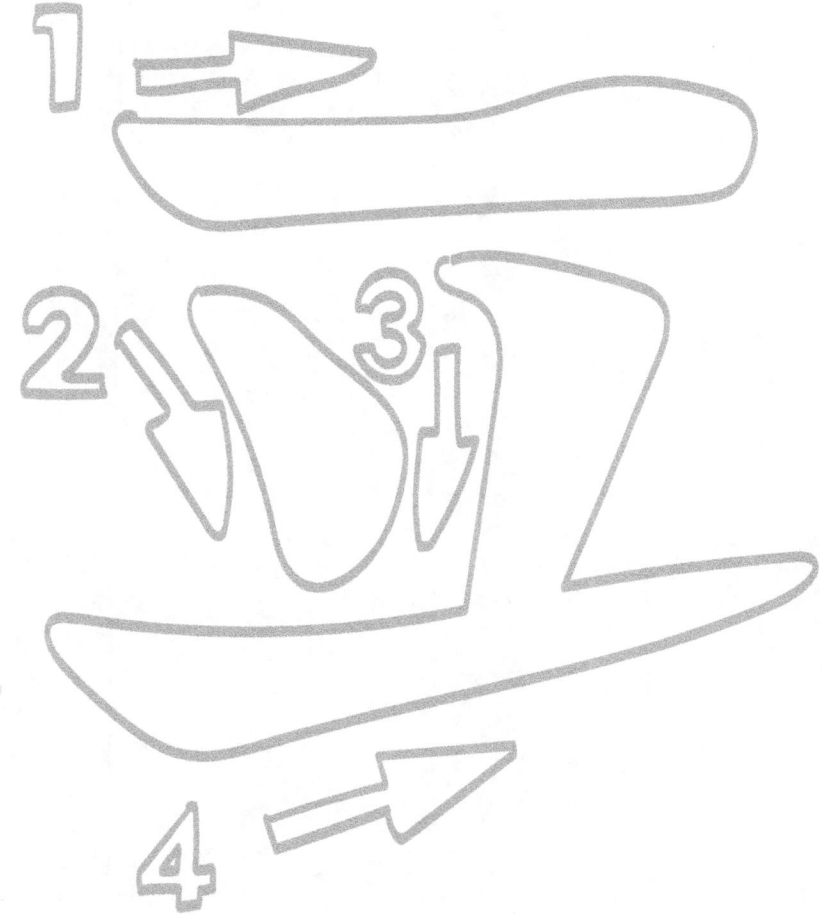

Practice writing the letter 10 times

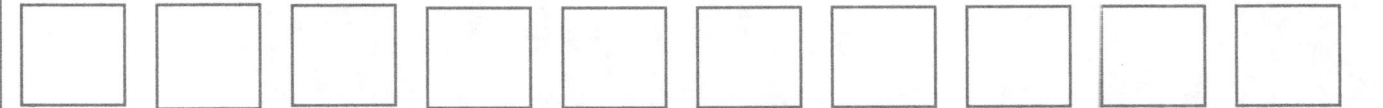

Pronounced hiut
Written in English as h

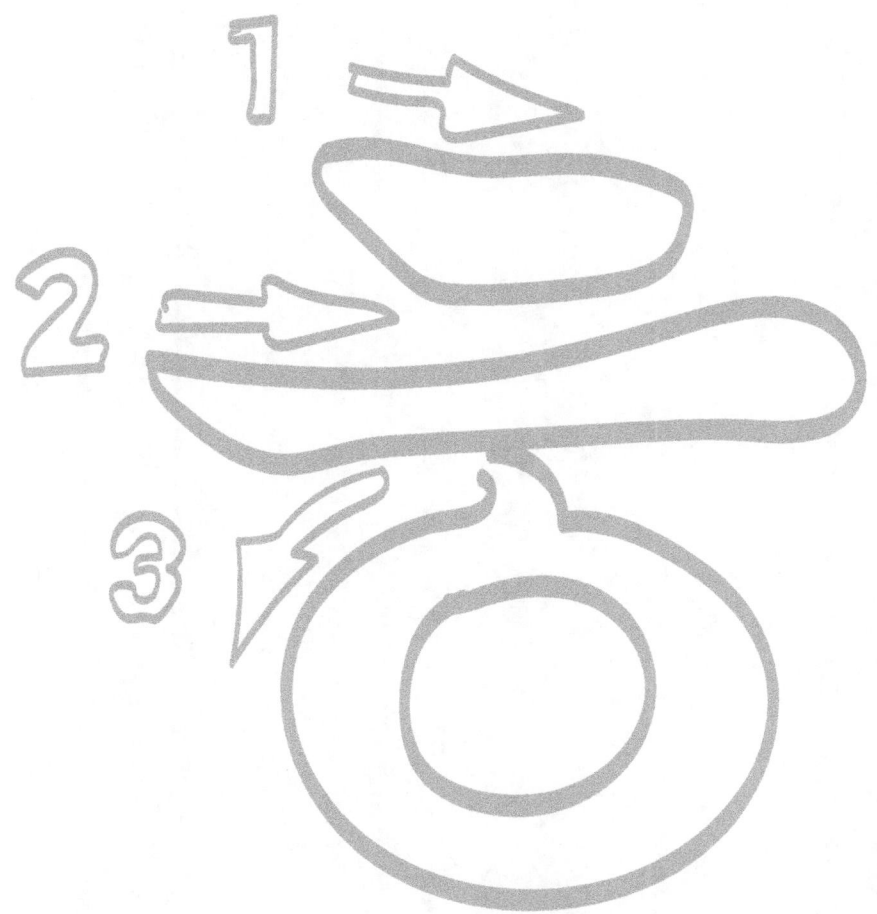

Practice writing the letter 10 times

Pronounced "ah"
Written in English as "a"

Practice writing the letter 10 times

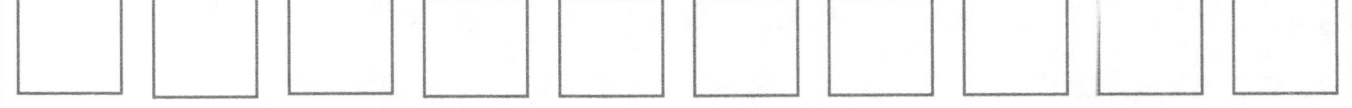

Pronounced "yah"
Written in English as "ya"

Practice writing the letter 10 times

Pronounced "oh"
Written in English as "o"

Practice writing the letter 10 times

Pronounced "yeo"
Written in English as "yo"

Practice writing the letter 10 times

Pronounced "u"
Written in English as "u"

Practice writing the letter 10 times

Pronounced "yu"
Written in English as "yu"

Practice writing the letter 10 times

Pronounced "eu"
Written in English "eu"

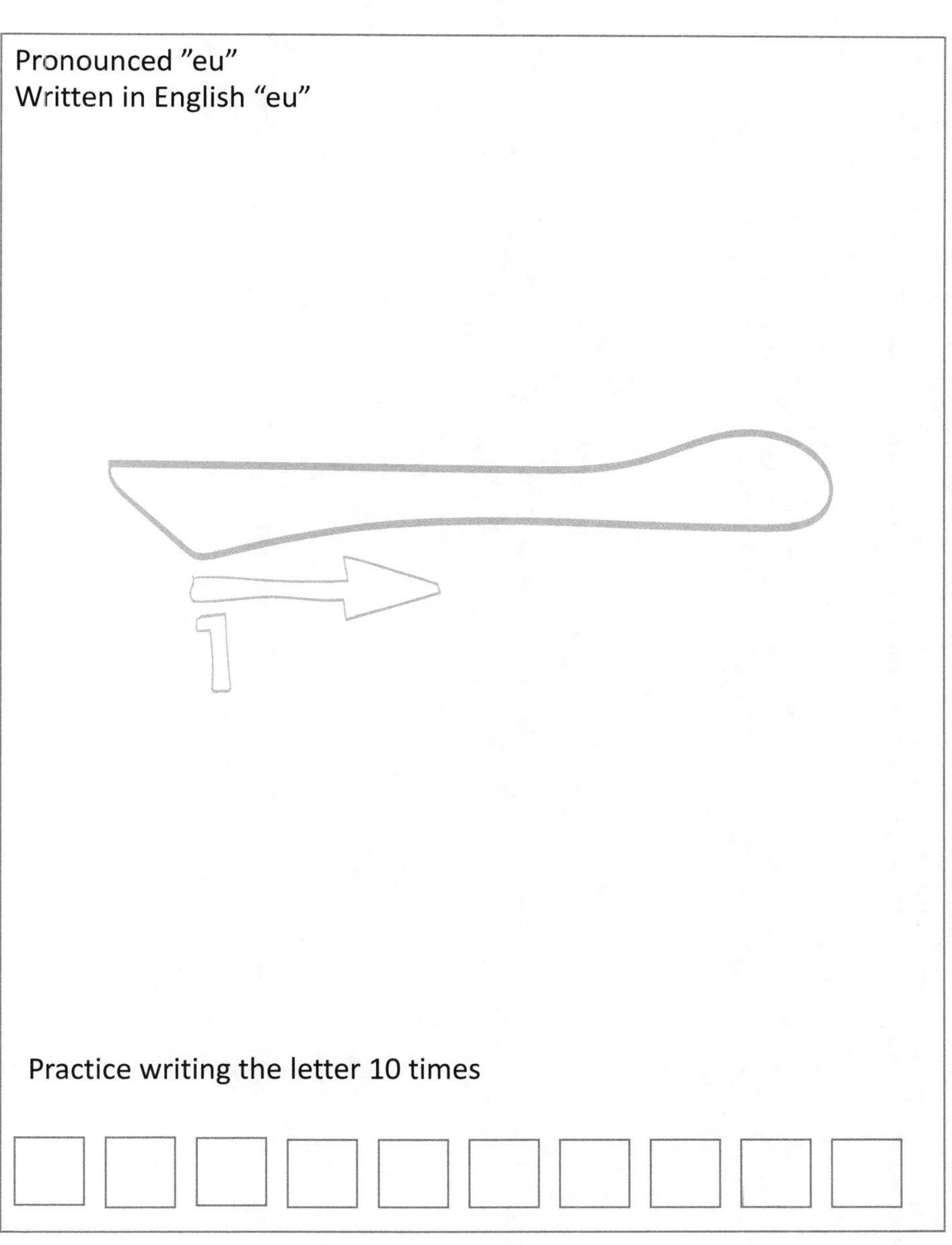

Practice writing the letter 10 times

Pronounced "ee"
Written in English as "I"

Practice writing the letter 10 times

Pronounced "o"
Written in English as "o"

Practice writing the letter 10 times

Pronounced "yu"
Written in English yu

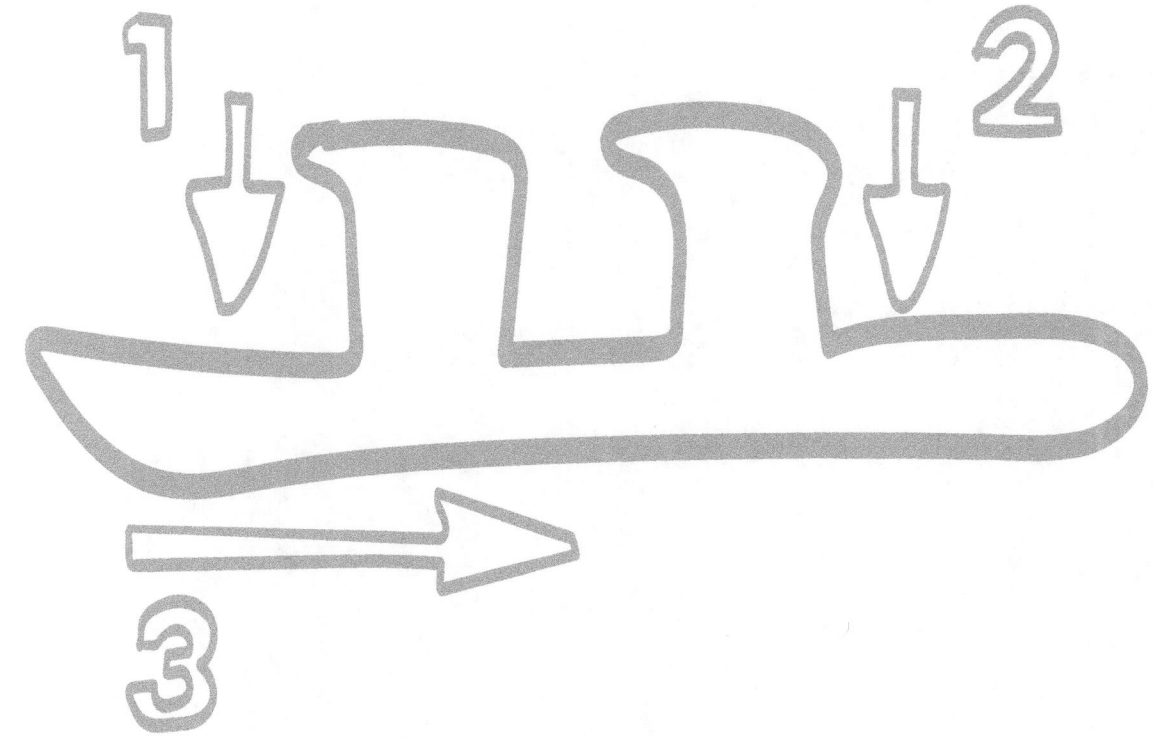

Practice writing the letter 10 times

Thank you for coloring and learning Korean.

Coming soon
Study and Color Korean numbers